# Michigan Activity Book

by Paula Ellis

illustrated by Anna Kaiser

Cover and book design by Jonathan Norberg

10 9 8 7 6 5
Copyright 2009 by Paula Ellis
Published by Adventure Publications
An imprint of AdventureKEEN
820 Cleveland Street South
Cambridge, Minnesota 55008
(800) 678-7006
www.adventurepublications.net
Printed in China

ISBN: 978-1-59193-226-0

W9-BGJ-774

# WELCOME TO MICHIGAN!

Is this your first visit to Michigan or do you live here? I hope that you have fun exploring Michigan and all the exciting places you visit.

Use your Michigan Activity Book to find new and exciting things to see and do. Ask mom and dad the questions listed in the book and see if they know the answers.

Have a wonderful time in Michigan, the Great Lakes State!

# ABOUT MICHIGAN

Michigan was the 26th state admitted to the United States of America, and it was named after Lake Michigan. Its name comes from the Ojibwa word *"mishigami,"* which means "large water" or "large lake." After the glaciers receded thousands of years ago, they left behind two separate land masses, or peninsulas. A peninsula is a land mass surrounded on three sides by water. The Upper Peninsula is as large as Connecticut, Delaware, Massachusetts and Rhode Island combined. The Lower Peninsula is shaped like a mitten. Michigan's two peninsulas, the Upper and the Lower, were connected by the Mackinac Bridge in 1957.

Michigan is called the Great Lakes State because it is bordered by four of the five Great Lakes: Lake Superior, Lake Michigan, Lake Huron and Lake Erie. The only Great Lake that does not touch Michigan is Lake Ontario. In fact, Michigan has the most freshwater shoreline in the world. A person standing anywhere in Michigan is never more than 85 miles from one of the Great Lakes. Michigan is also an industrial and agricultural center. It is the automobile capital of the world and Michigan farmers produce many crops, including apples, cherries, beans, asparagus, potatoes and sugar beets. Michigan is also rich in minerals and supplies the nation with iron, copper, salt, gravel and cement.

Because of the Great Lakes and its inland waterways, Michigan is a commercial and sport fishing paradise. Michigan is sometimes even referred to as the Winter Water Wonderland, because Michigan is the largest state east of the Mississippi River and there is a lot of room for fun. Come visit Michigan.

# ABOUT THE AUTHOR

Paula Ellis grew up in a small town in central Michigan. She enjoys being a grandma, exploring the wilderness, traveling and watching her four grandchildren grow and learn about the world in which they live. She strives to encourage children of all ages to see and explore all of the fascinating things around them. She dedicates this book to her daughter Heather and her son Todd David, two of the greatest joys of her life.

Anna Kaiser is an illustrator who graduated from The Minneapolis College of Art and Design in 2008. Anna enjoys creating illustrations for children's books and sculpting clay animals. In fact, she is working on starting her own pet sculpture business. She currently lives in her home state of Wisconsin with her three beautiful goldfish Julia, Goliath and Spike. If you would like to see more of Anna's work, visit her website at www.annakaiser.net.

# MICHIGAN STATE SYMBOLS

The state fish is the Brook Trout.

The state stone is the Petoskey Stone.

The state flower is the Apple Blossom.

The state bird is the American Robin.

The state reptile is the Painted Turtle.

The state mammal is the White-tailed Deer.

The state wildflower is the Dwarf Lake Iris.

The state gem is Chlorastrolite (Green Star Stone).

The state tree is the White Pine.

The state fossil is the Mastodon.

# DID YOU KNOW . . .

- Michigan is the 10th largest state. It is 456 miles long and 386 miles wide.

- No matter where you stand in Michigan, you are never more than 85 miles from a Great Lake.

- Wherever you are in Michigan, you are no farther than 6 miles from a lake or stream.

- Michigan has 11,037 lakes.

- Detroit is the largest city in Michigan.

- Lansing is the capital of Michigan.

- Michigan was the 26th state. It was granted statehood in 1837.

- Detroit is known as the car capital of the world.

- Gerald Ford, the 38th president of the United States, grew up in Michigan and was also an Eagle Scout.

- Michigan comes from the Ojibwa word *"mishigami*," meaning "large water" or "large lake."

- The Mackinac Bridge is 5 miles long, took 3 years to build and opened in 1957. It is sometimes called the "Mighty Mac."

- Battle Creek, Michigan, is home to the Kellogg and Post cereal companies and is known as the cereal capital of the world.

- The Detroit Zoo was the first zoo in America to eliminate animal cages.

- Michigan has the longest freshwater shoreline in the country.

- The French, English, Spanish and American flags have all flown over Michigan.

- The largest waterfall in Michigan is Tahquamenon Falls in the U.P.

- People in Michigan are called "Michiganders" not "Michiganians."

- You pronounce Mackinac "Mack–i–naw."

# APPLE BLOSSOM

The apple blossom is the state flower, and Michigan is known for its apples. There are apple orchards all over the state. Apple trees blossom in the spring and apples follow in the fall.

# BOAT

Michigan is surrounded by water, and many people enjoy boating on the Great Lakes or on Michigan's many inland lakes, rivers and streams. People use all sorts of boats, too, including houseboats, speedboats, fishing boats, and smaller boats like kayaks, paddleboats, and canoes.

# BRIDGES

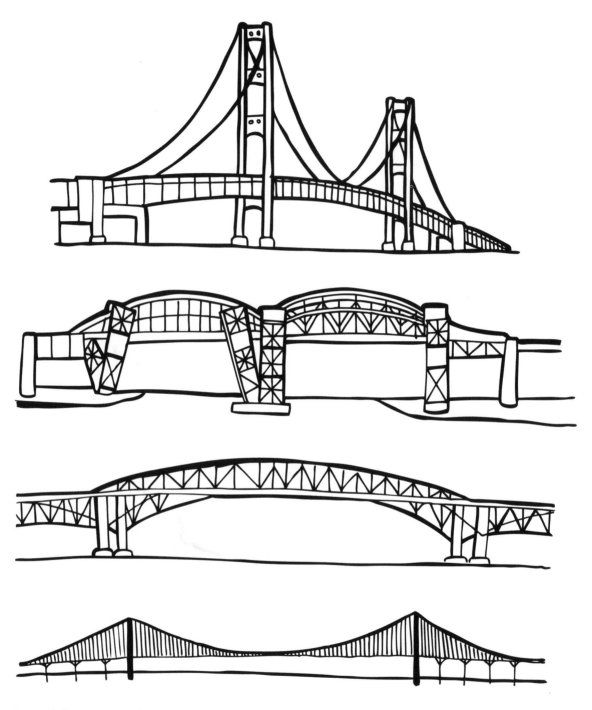

The Mackinac Bridge in Mackinaw City connects the Upper Peninsula to the Lower Peninsula. Three bridges connect Michigan to Canada: the International Bridge in Sault St. Marie, the Bluewater Bridge in Port Huron and the Ambassador Bridge in Detroit.

# CANOE

Many people enjoy canoeing on Michigan's lakes and rivers, and towns often host their own canoe races. One of the longest and most popular canoe races in Michigan is the AuSable Canoe Race, from Grayling to Oscoda. It is 120 miles long.

# CEREAL CITY

Battle Creek, Michigan, is also known as "Cereal City," and is home to Kellogg's and Post, two major breakfast cereal manufacturers in the U.S. If you eat breakfast cereal in the morning, there's a good chance that your breakfast cereal comes from Michigan.

# CHERRIES

Michigan is known for its cherries. In fact, Michigan produces more tart cherries than any other state, and it produces many sweet cherries as well. Traverse City is even referred to as the "Cherry Capital of the World."

# DETROIT

Detroit is the largest city in Michigan. Its reputation as the car capital of the world is long standing and has been based on three major companies: General Motors, Chrysler and Ford. Known as "The Big Three," these companies have employed many people in Michigan and around the world for decades.

# DOWNHILL SKIING

Many people enjoy downhill skiing in Michigan. There are ski resorts all over the state with hills available for those of all ages and abilities. Skiing is a fun way to enjoy the snow in Michigan.

# DUNES

Michigan has many beaches, and some of them have dunes, or large hills of sand piled up by the wind. The western shore of Michigan has some of the highest freshwater dunes in the world. Some, like the Sleeping Bear Dunes and Silver Lake Dunes, are popular tourist sites. You can ride on them in dune buggies, or you can climb to the top.

# EDISON

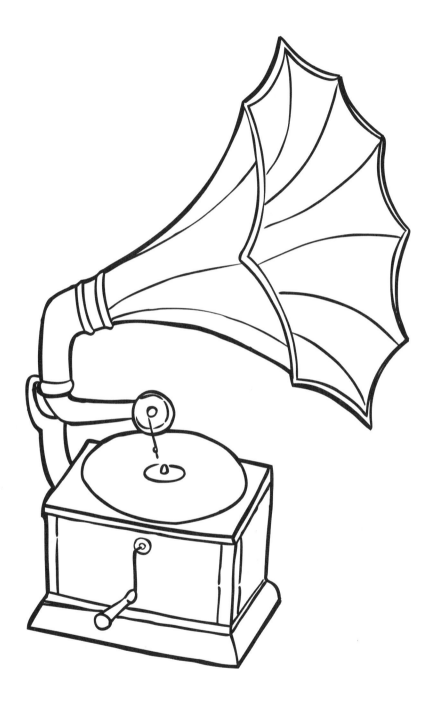

Thomas Alva Edison was an American inventor who grew up in Port Huron, Michigan. He is credited with many inventions we use today, including the electric light bulb and the phonograph (record player). His laboratory was moved from Menlo Park, New Jersey, and is now a part of Greenfield Village in Dearborn, Michigan.

# FLAG

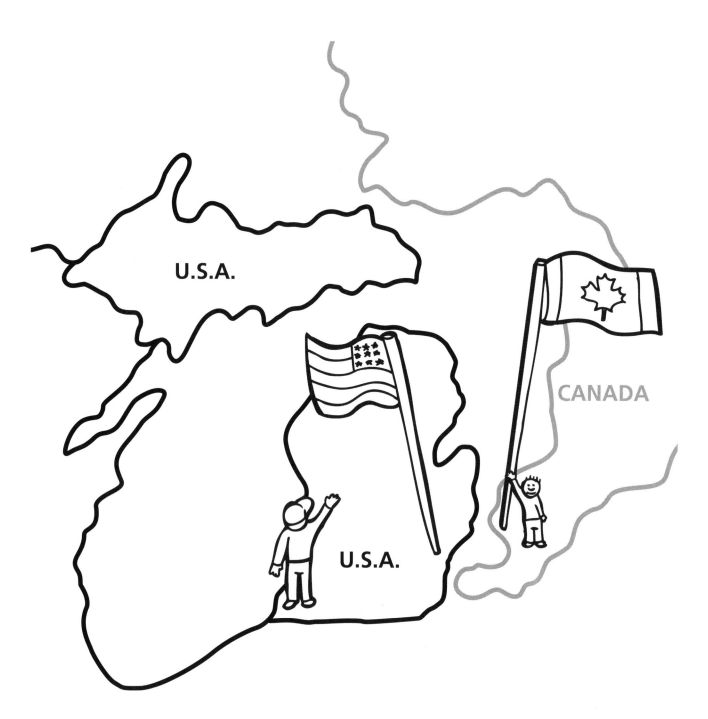

You may see the Canadian flag along the borders of Michigan. Canada borders Michigan to the north and to the east. In fact, Detroit, Michigan is actually north of Windsor, Ontario, which is part of Canada.

# FORD

Henry Ford was an inventor and built automobiles in Detroit, Michigan. His company, the Ford Motor Company, helped popularize the assembly line and changed how American factories made products. Ford's company began manufacturing the Model T in 1908.

# GERALD FORD

Gerald R. Ford was the 38th president of the United States of America and served from 1974-1977. He was raised in Grand Rapids, Michigan; the airport and a Presidential library are named in his honor. Like all Presidents, he flew in a special plane called *Air Force One*.

# GRAND HOTEL

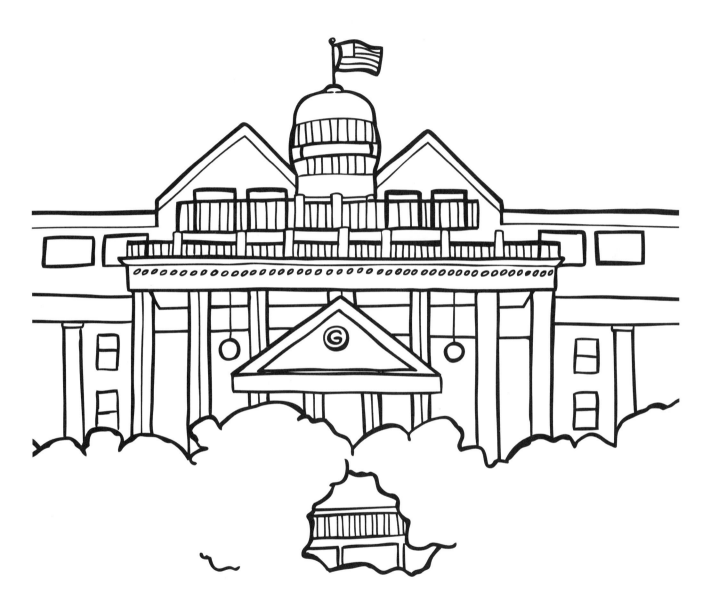

The Grand Hotel is located on Mackinac Island in Lake Huron. It is the largest summer resort hotel in the country and has the largest porch in the world. On a clear day, you can see the hotel from the Mackinac Bridge or Mackinaw City. Ferry boats transport visitors to the island, but you won't find any cars here, as they are forbidden. Instead, people get around by horse and carriage and bicycle.

# GREAT LAKES

Michigan is called the Great Lakes State and is bordered to the west by Lake Michigan, to the east by Lake Huron, to the north by Lake Superior and to the southeast by Lake Erie. The other Great Lake is Lake Ontario, but it does not touch Michigan. Michigan has more shoreline than any other state except Alaska.

# HENRY FORD MUSEUM

The Henry Ford is the largest indoor-outdoor museum complex in the country. Many of Ford's inventions are found in the museum, along with many historical items as well as relocated historical sites like the Wright Brothers' Bicycle Shop and Thomas Edison's laboratory.

# HOLLAND

Holland, Michigan, is on the shore of Lake Michigan. The city was founded by Dutch immigrants and is famous for the tulip festival it holds in May each year. The festival features over six million tulips and a number of activities and events related to the city's Dutch heritage.

# HORSE

One of the most popular islands in Michigan is Mackinac Island. You can only get there by boat, plane or by traveling across the ice in the winter, and cars are forbidden on the island. Horses pull carriages and wagons to take people and supplies around the island.

# ISLAND

There are many islands in the Great Lakes around Michigan. The most visited island is Mackinac Island. It is located in Lake Huron between the Upper and Lower Peninsulas. Other popular islands to visit are Beaver Island, Drummond Island and Isle Royale.

# ISLE ROYALE

Isle Royale is a wilderness island in northwestern Lake Superior. It is part of Michigan, but you can only get there by boat. Many wolves, moose, and other wild animals live on Isle Royale.

# JIFFY

Jiffy™, a food mix company, sells its products in the "little blue box." Jiffy makes its products in Chelsea, Michigan. The company began in 1930 and has become world-famous for its cake mixes, muffin mixes, pizza and pie crusts, and brownie and pancake mixes. They make over a million boxes of mix a day.

# JUMP

Skydiving is a popular sport in Michigan, and there are skydiving centers all over the state. Skydivers jump out of an airplane wearing a parachute and fall freely for a short period before floating back to earth. While falling, a skydiver can reach over a hundred miles per hour and can see the ground from thousands of feet up.

# KAYAK

Michigan is surrounded by water and has many lakes and rivers. Many people enjoy kayaking in Michigan, and many famous paddlers, including Olympic gold medalists, have come from Michigan.

# LANSING

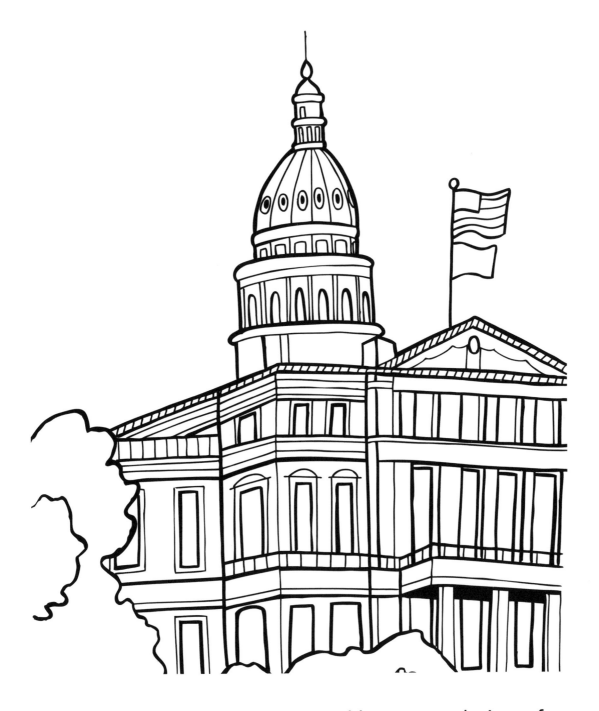

Lansing is the capital of Michigan and has a population of over 100,000. Located in the Lower Peninsula, Lansing is about 80 miles from Detroit. Construction of the State Capitol building was completed in 1879.

# LIGHTHOUSE

There are 124 lighthouses and navigational lights in Michigan. Whitefish Point Lighthouse is the oldest active lighthouse on Lake Superior. Active for over 150 years, it is located on Whitefish Point in the Upper Peninsula.

# MACKINAC BRIDGE

The Mackinac Bridge is 5 miles long and 552 feet above the water at the center. It connects the Upper and Lower Peninsulas of Michigan. Be sure to look all around, as you may see a freighter taking coal to Chicago or one heading toward Detroit. Mackinac is a French word, but the British, who occupied the Michigan mainland, spelled it "Mackinaw." The bridge and Mackinac Island are spelled Mackinac and the city is spelled Mackinaw City. Both words are pronounced: Mack-in-aw.

# NICKNAME

A common nickname for Michigan is "The Wolverine State," and the University of Michigan's athletic teams are known as the Wolverines. Michigan State University's athletic teams are called the Spartans. Both schools have produced many professional athletes and Olympians.

# ORE BOATS

Ore boats are commonly seen on the Great Lakes. They carry iron ore, coal, grain, cement and supplies throughout the lakes and harbors of Michigan. Ore boats are also called lake freighters.

# PENINSULA

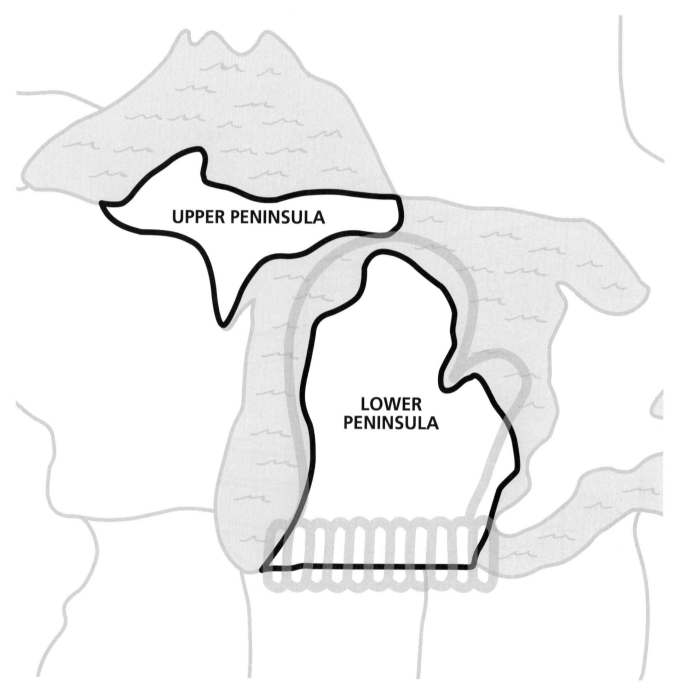

UPPER PENINSULA

LOWER PENINSULA

Michigan is made up of two peninsulas. (A peninsula is a piece of land surrounded by water on three sides.) They are called the Upper Peninsula and the Lower Peninsula. The Lower Peninsula is shaped like a mitten. If you hold your right hand up with the palm facing you, you have a map of the Lower Peninsula on your hand.

# PETOSKEY STONE

Petoskey stones are fossils of ancient corals. They are most often found along Lake Michigan and Lake Huron. The Petoskey Stone is the official stone of Michigan.

# PICTURED ROCKS

There are many beautiful places on Michigan's Upper Peninsula, especially in areas near Lake Superior's rocky shore. Pictured Rocks National Lakeshore, in Munising, Michigan, is a good example of this. Many people hike here to enjoy the unique, beautiful setting.

# QUADRICYCLE

The quadricycle was first made by Henry Ford. It is called a quadri-cycle because it was built on four bicycle tires and it was propelled by a gasoline engine. Ford first drove the quadricycle on June 4, 1896 and it was one of the vehicles that helped make the Ford Motor Company a success.

# RIVERS

Michigan has over 36,000 miles of rivers and streams, and they are home to many kinds of fish, birds, and other animals. Visitors and residents use them to fish, paddle, canoe and kayak, as well as for transportation and the generation of hydroelectric power.

# SNOW

Children and adults enjoy Michigan's winter and all the snow that falls here. In Keweenaw County in the Upper Peninsula, 390 inches of snow fell during the winter of 1978–79! That's 32½ feet deep. Snow days are another reason kids in Michigan like winter; when the weather becomes too bad, school is closed.

# SOO BOAT LOCKS

Lake Superior is higher than Lake Huron, so big boats use the Soo Boat Locks to travel between Lake Superior and the lower Great Lakes. A boat enters the locks and a gate closes behind it. The water level in the lock either raises or lowers; this raises or lowers the boat to the lake level on the other side and helps the boats go on their way.

# SNOWMOBILE

Snowmobiles are a great way to see Michigan in winter. Snowmobile trails crisscross the state and can be found on both the Upper and Lower Peninsulas. There are even famous snowmobile races held in the state.

# TURTLE

The Painted Turtle is the state reptile of Michigan, and during the summer they are easy to spot sunbathing on logs or rocks. They are called painted turtles because of the brightly colored and patterned undersides of their shells.

# TAHQUAMENON FALLS

Tahquamenon Falls is in the Upper Peninsula of Michigan. It has an upper falls and a lower falls. The upper falls are 200 feet across and it is the second largest waterfall east of the Mississippi River, after Niagara Falls.

# UNDERGROUND

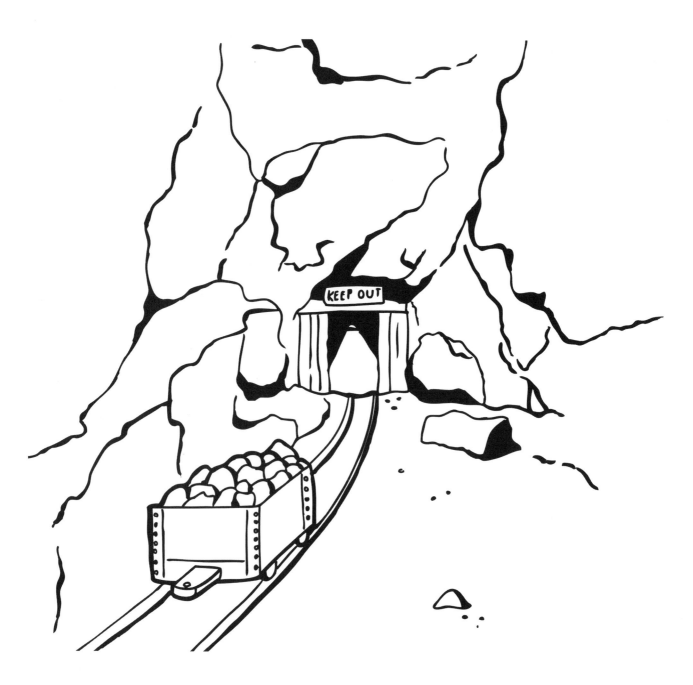

There are over 800 underground mines in Michigan. Miners in Michigan work underground to find iron ore, copper, gold, limestone, salt and coal.

# VERNORS™

Vernors™ Ginger Ale was first made in Detroit, Michigan by James Vernor in 1866. Vernors™ shares the title of "America's oldest soft drink" with Hires Root Beer. Drinking Vernors™ often makes you sneeze or cough because of all the bubbles.

# WEATHER

EDMUND FITZGERALD

Michigan is surrounded by large bodies of water. This makes the land colder in the summer and warmer in the winter. This can help create storms, especially during certain seasons; these storms have caused many shipwrecks.

# WILDFLOWER

The Dwarf Lake Iris is Michigan's state wildflower. It is native to the state but is an endangered species. The Dwarf Lake Iris grows only in the Great Lakes area and most of the world's population of this iris is found in Michigan.

# WOODS

The state tree of Michigan is the white pine. The white pine has a cluster of five needles; the needles are 3–5 inches long. Bald eagles like to build their nests in white pines. There are four National Forests in Michigan where you can see them: Hiawatha National Forest, Ottawa National Forest, Manistee National Forest, and Huron National Forest.

# X MARKS THE SPOT

Buried treasure—gold—was first discovered in Ishpeming, Michigan in Marquette County in 1845. Gold has also been found in small amounts in rivers and streams in both the Upper and Lower Peninsulas.

# YOOPER

People in the Upper Peninsula proudly call themselves "Yoopers." Yoopers are hard-working people who enjoy the solitude that the U.P. has to offer and the outdoor recreation that is available in the U.P.

# ZERO

In the winter, the weather can get very cold in Michigan. The temperature often drops below zero, and the record cold temperature in Michigan is 51 degrees below zero, set on February 4, 1934 in Vanderbilt.

# ZOO

There are several zoos in Michigan. One of the largest is the Detroit Zoo. It is located in Royal Oak, Michigan, and was the first zoo in the United States to have open, natural exhibits. Another popular Michigan zoo is the John Ball Zoo in Grand Rapids. Visit the zoo and see all the wonderful animals, reptiles, birds and flowers.

# FILL IN THE BLANKS

M  _ _ _ _ _ _

_ _ _ _ I _ _ _ _ _

_ _ C _ _ _ _

_ H _ _ _ _ _ _

_ _ _ I _

_ _ _ _ G _

_ _ _ A _   _ _ _ _ _

_ _ N _ _ _ _

1. What is the shape of Michigan? (pg. 34)

2. What is the Lower or Upper part of Michigan called? (pg. 34)

3. What bridge connects Lower Michigan to Upper Michigan? (pg. 31)

4. What tasty red fruit is from Michigan? (pg. 11)

5. What is the state bird of Michigan? (pg. 4)

6. What connects the two Peninsulas? (pg. 8)

7. What bodies of water surround the state of Michigan? (pg. 20)

8. What is the capital of Michigan? (pg. 29)

# CAN YOU NAME THE MAMMALS IN MICHIGAN?

5. mos

1. wolf

2. skavel-

6. fox

3. hover

7. ber

4. dere

8. skent

# WORD FIND

```
F  O  D  R  R  L  A  K  E  S  H  L
O  R  E  M  A  C  K  I  N  A  C  C
M  T  T  P  N  G  F  O  R  D  D  H
J  U  R  D  S  B  R  I  D  G  E  E
I  R  O  B  I  N  F  C  J  L  R  R
F  T  I  A  N  I  O  L  T  O  R  R
F  L  T  I  G  E  R  S  W  G  I  E
Y  E  H  E  A  T  H  E  R  S  E  E
L  I  S  L  A  N  D  C  A  R  S
```

DETROIT        MACKINAC        ORE

BRIDGE         ROBIN           FORD

CARS           LANSING         LOGS

TIGERS         CHERRIES        TURTLE

LAKES          ISLAND          JIFFY

# CONNECT THE DOTS

Connect the dots and find the largest mammal in the state of Michigan.

# WHAT DOES NOT BELONG IN MICHIGAN?

# WORD FIND

```
C J Z W C O U G A R E R
H O J S O M S O R P I A
I A L M W L Q A O L F B
P N B E A R U T D D M B
M U T E J P I G J E O I
U W O L V E R I N E O T
N O M K T S R H O R S E
K L T O D D E P K W E H
A F O X C T L D A V I D
```

| DEER | COUGAR | BEAR |
|------|--------|------|
| MOOSE | RABBIT | WOLF |
| CHIPMUNK | SQUIRREL | PIG |
| HORSE | WOLVERINE | COW |
| FOX | ELK | GOAT |

# FRUIT

PEACHES

CHERRIES

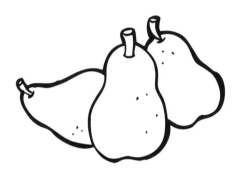

PEARS

BLUEBERRIES

STRAWBERRIES

APPLES

RASPBERRIES

Michigan grows many different fruits.

# MAKE A MAP OF MICHIGAN

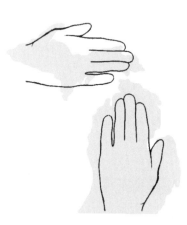

Place your left hand palm up at the top of the page with your fingers pointing right. Trace your hand. Then, place your left hand palm down in the middle of the page with your fingers pointing up and trace your hand again. Then, color in your map of Michigan.

# QUESTIONS

1. What is the capital of Michigan? __ __ __ __ __ __ __

2. What are the names of the five Great Lakes? __ __ __ __,

   __ __ __ __ __ __ __ __, __ __ __ __ __ __ __,

   __ __ __ __ __ __ __ __, __ __ __ __ __

3. Who is the only president to come from Michigan?

   __ __ __ __ __ __   __ __ __ __

4. What is the state bird of Michigan? __ __ __ __ __

5. What is the state flower of Michigan?

   __ __ __ __ __   __ __ __ __ __ __ __

6. What is the town where cereal is made?

   __ __ __ __ __ __   __ __ __ __ __

7. What is the name of the bridge that connects the Upper and Lower Peninsula?

   __ __ __ __ __ __ __ __   __ __ __ __ __ __

8. What is the largest city in Michigan? __ __ __ __ __ __ __

9. What is the name of the biggest waterfall in Michigan?

   __ __ __ __ __ __ __ __ __ __   __ __ __ __ __

10. What is the country that borders Michigan? __ __ __ __ __ __

# MAZE

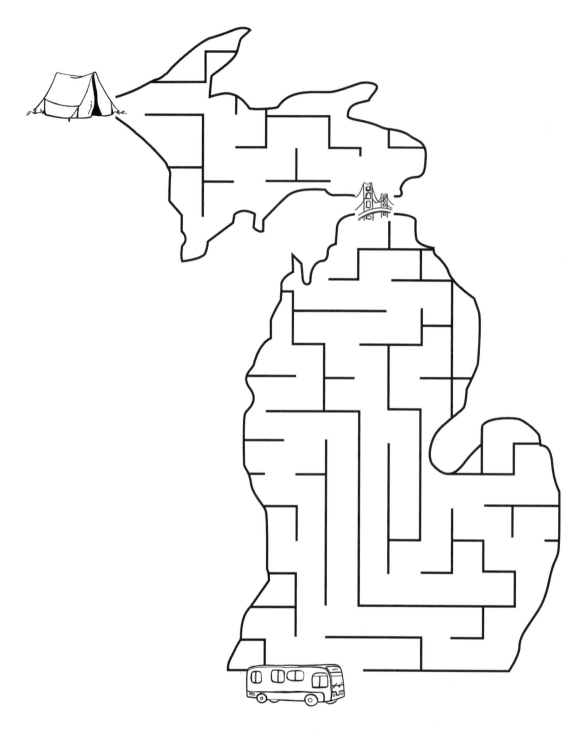

Get the campers to their campground in the Upper Peninsula of Michigan.

# ANSWER PAGE

## Page 53–Fill In The Blanks

1. Mitten
2. Peninsula
3. Mackinac
4. Cherries
5. Robin
6. Bridge
7. Great Lakes
8. Lansing

## Page 54–Can You Name The Mammals in Michigan?

1. Wolf
2. Squirrel
3. Beaver
4. White-tailed Deer
5. Moose
6. Fox
7. Black Bear
8. Skunk

## Page 55–Word Find

```
F O D R (L A K E S) H L
(O R E (M A C K I N A C)
 M T T P N G (F O R D) H
 J U R D S (B R I D G E)
 I (R O B I N) F C J L R
 F T I A N I O L T O R
 F L (T I G E R S) W G I
 Y E H E A T H E R S E
 L (I S L A N D)(C A R S)
```

## Page 57–What Does Not Belong in Michigan

# ANSWER PAGE

## Page 58–Word Find

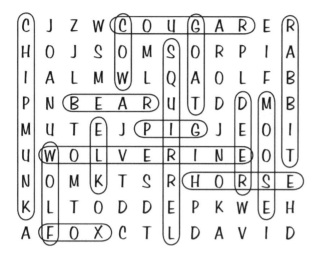

## Page 61–Questions

1. Lansing
2. Erie, Michigan, Ontario, Superior, Huron
3. Gerald Ford
4. Robin
5. Apple Blossom
6. Battle Creek
7. Mackinac Bridge
8. Detroit
9. Tahquamenon Falls
10. Canada

## Page 62–Maze

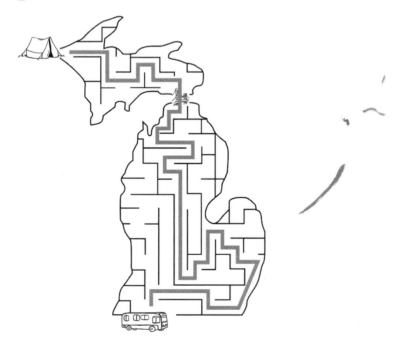